POCKET IMAGES

Hucknall
& District

The poet Lord Byron is buried in Hucknall Parish church. He was described by Shelley as 'The Pilgrim of Eternity'. (David Henshaw)

POCKET IMAGES

Hucknall & District

Harry Smith

NONSUCH

First published 2003
This new pocket edition 2007
Images unchanged from first edition

Nonsuch Publishing Limited
Cirencester Road, Chalford,
Stroud, Gloucestershire, GL6 8PE
www.nonsuch-publishing.com

Nonsuch Publishing is an imprint of NPI Media Group

© Harry Smith, 2003

The right of Harry Smith to be identified as the Author
of this work has been asserted in accordance with the
Copyrights, Designs and Patents Act 1988.

All rights reserved. No part of this book may be reprinted
or reproduced or utilised in any form or by any electronic,
mechanical or other means, now known or hereafter invented,
including photocopying and recording, or in any information
storage or retrieval system, without the permission in writing
from the Publishers.

British Library Cataloguing in Publication Data.
A catalogue record for this book is available from the British Library.

ISBN 978-1-84588-396-6

Typesetting and origination by Nonsuch Publishing Limited
Printed in Great Britain by Oaklands Book Services Limited

Contents

	Introduction	7
	Acknowledgements	8
1.	Hucknall Town	9
2.	Civic Education and Religion	27
3.	Work and Industry	45
4.	Events and Personalities	57
5.	Sports and Leisure in the District	73
6.	Hucknall RAF and Rolls Royce	83
7.	Around Hucknall, Papplewick, Linby and Annesley	95
8.	Around Hucknall, Newstead and the Abbey	109
9.	Around Hucknall, Bulwell and Beauvale Abbey	121

Above: A typical scene in Hucknall Market Place, demonstrating the hustle and bustle of a Friday-morning market which has been held since 1874. An average of eighty stall-holders occupy space each week.

Left: This is how Hucknall church appeared when Lord Byron was interred in 1824. (David Henshaw)

Introduction

Hucknall today is vastly changed from the one I was born into in 1910. The town for me began at my parents' house on Titchfield Street, adjoining the factory which housed the family business, and manufactured knitted lace which is still sold today. The Hucknall Manufacturing Company was founded by my grandfather in 1863 and the craft of shawl and sock manufacture was, apart from farming, the primary mode of employment until the sinking of the coal mines in 1861.

My early years were spent and enjoyed in vibrant Hucknall, which the coal industry and associated companies helped to create both socially and commercially. The swimming baths generously gifted to the town by Edward Ellis in 1909 were a great attraction for many, myself included, whilst the Empire theatre in Vine Terrace and the Scala cinema on Annesley Road were considered excellent venues for entertainment.

Excursions to Nottingham were made simple with the facilities provided by two railway companies, the LNER and LMS, both providing a more than an ample service. The railways in the early part of the twentieth century were a means of transport for a large number of female workers who commuted daily from Hucknall to work in the city of Nottingham's textile industry. This daily exodus changed dramatically when Mr George Spencer, then of Lutterworth, came to the town and purchased land to erect his new Vedonis factory for the manufacture of ladies' undergarments. The building of a new Viyella factory, producing shirts for gentlemen, also provided work for hundreds of local girls.

In 1926 the Hucknall Rotary Club was founded. I was privileged to have been a past member and president, and it is a tribute to its founders that it is still active and continues its service to the community today.

The 1930s brought some distress to the district. Hucknall had more than 1,000 unemployed and many workers on short time. Recovery was slow, but also a time of change. Poor housing was cleared, new estates were built and town improvements began.

The 1939–45 War brought the conflict close to the population with frequent air-raid warnings and the presence of HM Forces in the form of RAF and Army personnel.

The town had its own Home Guard, Observer Corps, Special Constables, Air Raid Wardens, Fire Watchers and every street had its own ARP Warden.

The end of the war saw the return of elections in the town and surrounding district, with the Labour Party gaining control and retaining a firm grip until the very recent elections.

1974 saw the end of the Hucknall Urban District Council on which both my father, W. Calladine, and I served for many years, autonomy passing to the Ashfield District Council where it remains to this day.

The closing of the collieries and manufacturing industries led to redundancies and early retirement for many employees. Today there is such speed of change that it seems everything is altering: highways, public buildings, houses, shops and factories all stand on former colliery sites—the list is endless and all trace of a great industry has disappeared for ever.

I am especially pleased to have been invited to write the introduction to this book. Harry Smith and I have shared a common interest in local history and enjoyed a friendship over many years. The success of his previous publication *Hucknall Looking Back* will, I am sure, be repeated in *Hucknall and District* and will add in no small measure to the history of the town.

Harold Francis Calladine
Former Mayor of Gedling
1975-1976

Acknowledgements

Grateful thanks are due to the following friends: Joan Bullock, Richard Bullock, Maureen Dixon, Andy Hamilton, The Revd Tom Irvine, Geoff Breedon, Jack Darrington, Philip Smith, Jack Cooper, Howard Marshall, and Julie Tasker for the loan of family photographs.

Special thanks to David Henshaw for providing the drawings, and Ann for her computer skills.

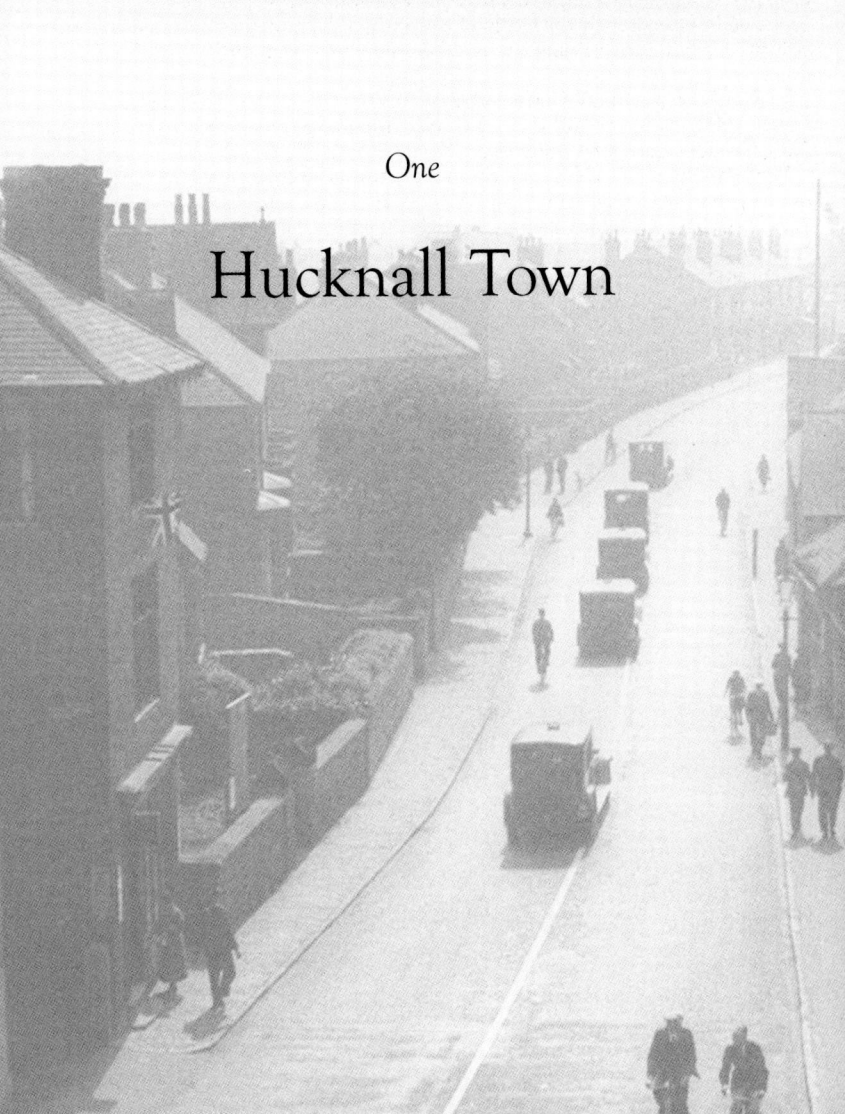

One

Hucknall Town

A quiet scene of Hucknall High Street. On the right, the petrol pumps of the Central Garage (which is now domiciled on Papplewick Lane), can be seen under the RAC sign.

Looking down Portland Road from the roof of the Byron cinema. Rhodes shawl factory is on the immediate left, then Calladines fish and chip shop. The old Hucknall Police Station is on the right of the picture.

An early Trent bus wends its way through the Hucknall carnival crowd in the 1930s. Pat Griffin's barber shop can clearly be seen. The sign on the bus optimistically indicates 'Nottingham Direct'.

Demolition almost completed in the High Street in the 1930s. The sight is now occupied by the chemist and post office. Behind the house pictured centre stands the Half Moon Hotel.

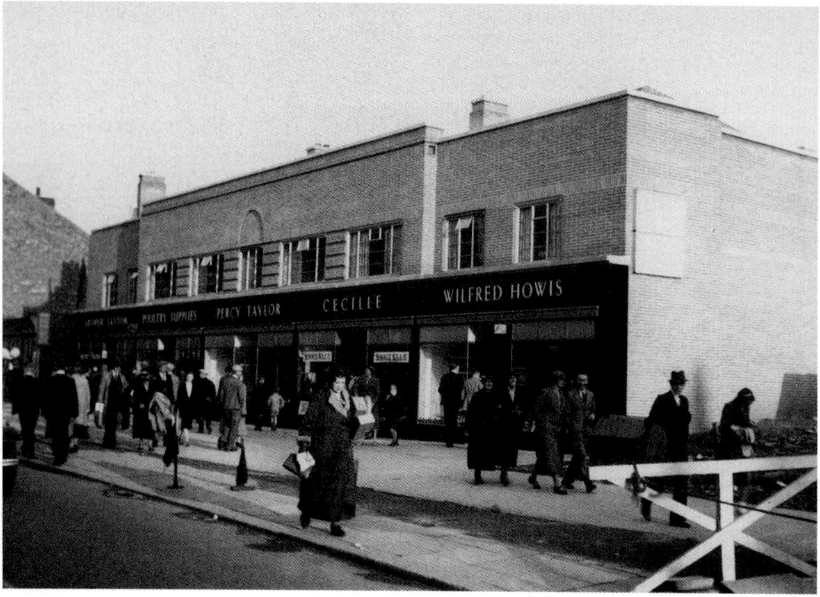
POULTRY SUPPLIES
PERCY TAYLOR
CECILLE
WILFRED HOWIS

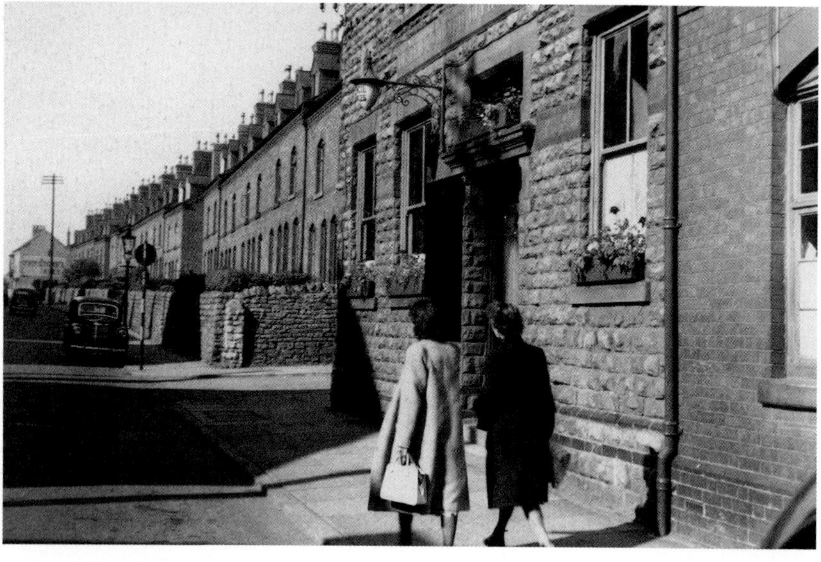

Opposite above: Pictured here are the first occupants of the new shops after road widening and demolition. The void on the right, which is now occupied by the post office, would have been the site of The Byrons Rest.

Opposite below: The old Hucknall Urban District Offices on Watnall Road in the 1960s. The entrance to the Council Yard can also been seen. Note the 'Beer-off' (meaning 'off licence' in the Hucknall area) in the far distance (since demolished), and the space now occupied by a wine shop.

Right: This cottage yard on Wood Lane would be typical of the rear of early dwellings in the town.

Below: Market Place, Hucknall, when car parking was free. Just seen on the extreme right is a sweet and tobacconist shop owned by the popular Hilda pepper, who traded in the town for many years.

Hucknall Market Place after market day, in the 1930s. Stallards shoe shop can be seen with the Half Moon Hotel towering behind. Notice the early bus standing outside the library. The ground apertures which held the stall uprights were typical of many market town provision for that purpose.

Baker Street corner, the final phase looking towards Annesley Road. The stone chimney was part of a blacksmiths forge which originally occupied the site.

Titchfield Park in the 1960s. The sight of the former boating lake, it is currently a children's play area and returns to something like its origins when torrential rain floods the area.

An early 1950s view of Portland Road, just below Bolsover Street. A site of persistent flooding for many years after heavy rain, this was only cured by a major road-work undertaking in the mid-1950s. The No. 61 Trent bus, pictured, terminated at Nottingham Mount Street–now a car park.

The Crown, Byron Street, Hucknall, just prior to demolition in the 1960s. The photographer's Mini just squeezes into the picture and gives a guide to the size of the building.

Byron Street, photographed from Watnall Road, all but gone. The Crown, shown in the previous picture, can be seen on the left.

Portland Farm, Portland Road, now the sight of a Further Education College. The Byron cinema can be seen in the background.

The Police Station on the corner of Duke Street and Portland Road. Sandbags are being delivered to complete the air raid precautions at the outbreak of war in September 1939.

Frank Sisson's window, High Street. This impressive window display was to advertise the Coronation of Queen Elizabeth II in 1953. Sales of televisions really took off after this occasion, most of them being supplied in the Hucknall area by Frank Sisson and Arthur Saxton.

Above: A very old photograph of Hucknall Parish church before extensions in 1887-88. The house abutting the east window of the church was the home of the Calladine family, one of whom witnessed the funeral of the poet Byron in 1824.

Below: Another old photograph showing the demolition of Manor Farm, Station Road, in the mid-1960s, marked the end of the Byron family link with this house. From the eighteenth century it was the home of the Daws Family and William Daws, steward to the fifth Lord Byron, died there in 1774. It is now a car park.

Wood Lane as it was before houses took over in the 1930s. This was the gateway to the Misk Hills Grandmothers Steps and the Blue Bell Wood. A favourite walk for Hucknall families on balmy summer evenings until the M1 motorway scythed through this delightful area.

Broomhill Cottages on Nottingham Road, taken before road widening in the 1950s.

This old photograph shows General Booth motoring through Baker Street, Hucknall, on 10 July 1908. 'X' presumably marks the General. The building on the left of the picture was the house of the Rate Collector J.H. Parkin.

Hucknall's one-horse snow plough in the 1930s. Snow is manually cleared on South Street while the Council horse waits patiently. The Library is on the right of the picture, while further along a lorry appears to be delivering beer to the Liberal Club.

Opposite above: The lake in Titchfield Park in the depths of winter. The large property in the centre is the Empire Club in Beardall Street.

Opposite below: Another winter scene; this time the ancient porch of Hucknall Parish church.

Right: These old stone cottages just off Annesley Road in Allen Street were known as Towel Roller Row.

Below: Broomhill Road Butlers Hill air raid shelters almost completed in 1939. St Johns Crescent and Butlers Hill School together with the Cigar Factory can be seen in the background.

Onlookers on Linby Lane wait to wave friends and relations off for a day out as the train leaves the Hucknall Midland Station in 1949.

Hucknall from the air. This aerial pictures shows the Central Railway Station (centre) and on the right the Vedonis works.

Byron Statue, Market Place, Hucknall, in better times taken shortly after being colourfully adorned with yellow hair much to the photographer's (Eric Morley) distaste.

Hucknall's most famous son, the composer Eric Coates was born at this house, No. 140 Watnall Road. Dr Coates, his wife and five children moved to Tenter Hill, Duke Street, when Eric was a small child. The splendid staircase, in one of the two semi-detached properties shown, suggests that the two houses at that time were one.

The Byron Window showing the family Coat of Arms—the Mermaid in the Ascendancy. This window was originally installed in the Public Hall, Watnall Road, in 1922 by the Byron Lodge of Freemasons. When the Public Hall was sold to private owners the window was removed and is now in private ownership.

The old Green Dragon, Watnall Road, in 1912, which states itself to be the only home-brewed house in Hucknall. On the death of the landlord in 1919 the premises were sold to Shipstones Brewery and demolished in 1925. The quality of the reproduction is indicative of its age.

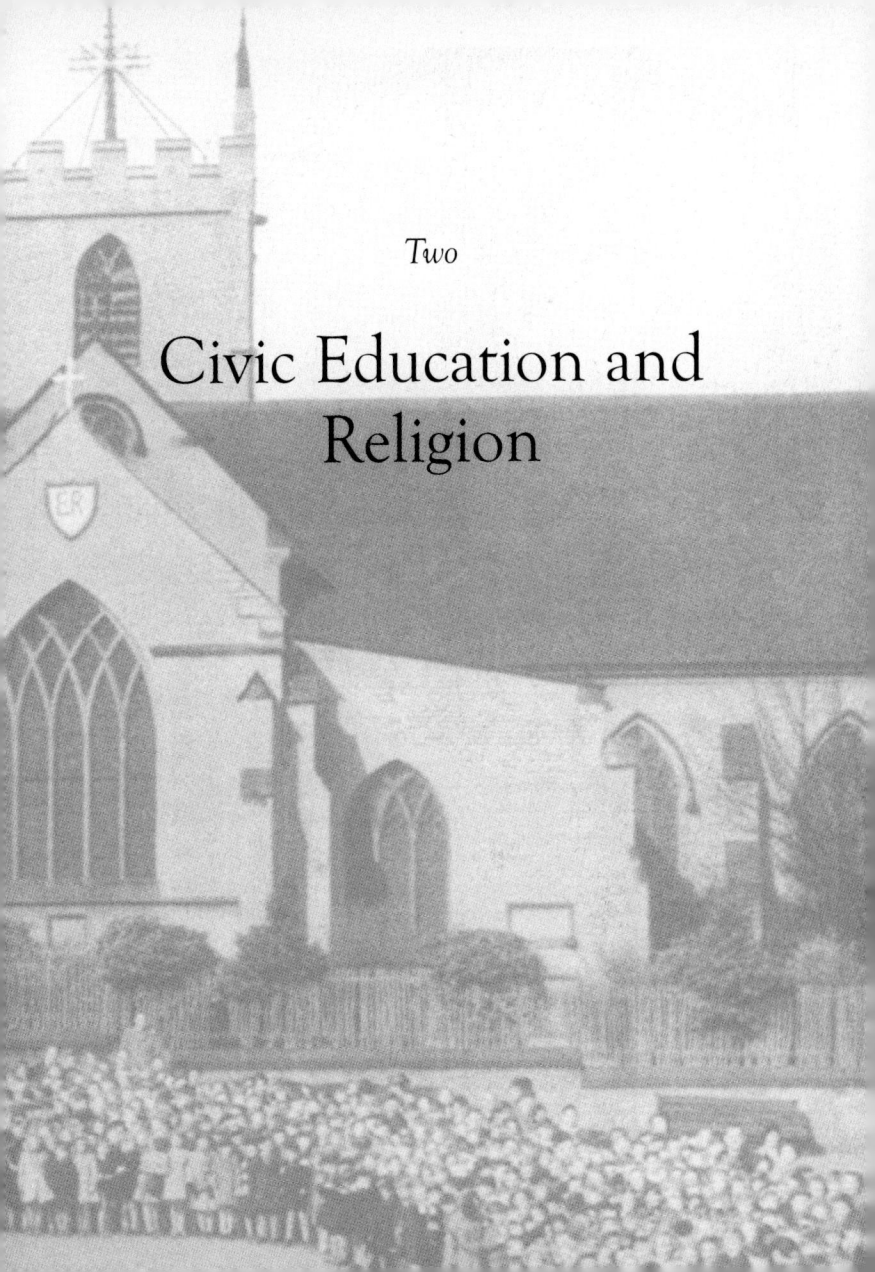

Two

Civic Education and Religion

Hucknall Urban District Council members and officials pictured on the Library steps in 1970. Back row, from left to right: Cllr Jack Barker, Clerk to the Council Harry Sharp, Treasurer Edward Thrall. Middle row: Councillors S. Grainger, Bernard Simms, George Smedley, Dick Bullock, Harold Calladine, ? Rhodes Surveyor, Cllr. Don Reynolds. Front row: Councillors Yvonne Turner, Chairman Jim Turner, Phylis Watson, J. Hayes, -?-, Jack Bingham, Eric Morley.

The ever popular and genial Richard (Dick) Bullock, a lifelong member of the Salvation Army who worked in the Hucknall coal mines. He was awarded the MBE for his devotion to public service, which culminated in his election as Chairman of Hucknall Urban District Council in 1964-1965. He served in the Second World War as an Army Sergeant and took part in the D-Day landings in 1944. Always with him was his Bible, marked at Joshua Chapter One, the reference ends: 'Be strong and of good courage'. He died suddenly in 1973, the year his son became Chairman of the old Hucknall Urban District Council.

Richard Hanson Bullock became Chairman of Hucknall Urban District Council in 1973, the year his father passed away. Richard is a practising solicitor with an established legal firm. In 1980 he was appointed Under-Sheriff for the City of Nottingham and more recently Derbyshire in the same capacity. His swearing in ceremonies were especially poignant as the Bible used was the one carried by his father in June 1944 when he landed in France with the French Canadian Force.

The year 1986 marked the centenary celebrations in Hucknall of the birth of the composer Eric Coates. The occasion was suitably marked with concerts in the City of Nottingham and Hucknall. This photograph shows the composer's son, Austin, being warmly applauded at the reception and exhibition at the Hucknall Library. With the author is the Chairman of Ashfield District Council with his lady.

Opposite above: Members of Hucknall Urban District Council and local dignitaries assemble outside the Council Offices in Watnall Road, 1937. The Hucknall Squadron of the RAF had suffered the loss of four of their airmen and the official party is shown here prior to parading to the Parish Church. In the centre of the doorway is Jim Goulding, Chairman, second from the left is Councillor H. Calladine, seventh from the left is Councillor Harry Johns, then Councillors G. Goodall and Wilf Reynolds. Second from the right is Joe Barker standing next to Mrs Northfield.

Opposite below: The Civic Party move off to the parish church. The Public Hall can clearly be seen, while further along Watnall Road is the old Wesleyan Chapel.

Former members of the Hucknall Urban District Council, which include Albert Brecknock, local librarian and Byron historian who wrote two books about the poet. Messrs Richard Gandy, Dr Garstang, Ira Buck, G. Goodall, Jack Radford, Charles Northfield.

Above: The Revd Canon Alan Haydock, pictured centre, was President of Hucknall Rotary Club in 1973. Formerly team vicar at St John's church, Hucknall, Canon Haydock moved to East Bridgford as priest in charge of that Parish. Known throughout the County of Nottinghamshire for his entertaining and witty after-dinner speeches, he formerly enjoyed cricket with Hucknall Cricket Club and was a keen supporter of Nottingham Forest and Notts County Football and Cricket Clubs, as well as being an accomplished amateur thespian. Rotarian Bernard Stallard stands extreme right, with Malcolm Granger, Chairman of Hucknall Round Table, immediately behind.

Right: Note the reference to the 'Public Baths'. These were provided twelve years later by the Rt Hon. John Edward Ellis as a gift to the town.

HUCKNALL TORKARD URBAN DISTRICT COUNCIL, 1898.

To the ELECTORS of HUCKNALL TORKARD, EAST WARD.

Ladies and Gentlemen,

We have been requested to offer ourselves as Candidates for this Ward at the ensuing Election of District Councillors, and have much pleasure in doing so.

The careful management of all matters relating to the Public Health of the Town will have our constant attention. The provision of Public Baths is, in our judgment, a matter pressing for decision. We trust it may be found possible in the immediate future to provide and manage Baths in a manner which will necessitate but a trifling expense to the Ratepayers.

A large supply of additional Allotments is required to satisfy the men of the Town. Believing as we do that such Allotments are very beneficial in many ways to those who occupy the Allotments, we shall do all in our power to increase their number.

We shall devote constant care to the supervision of the expenditure of your money, and whilst we shall study to promote in every way the interests and welfare of the Town we shall oppose any expenditure which is not clearly for the benefit of the inhabitants.

Yours faithfully,

Unionists

JOHN THORPE BARLOW.
GEORGE ROBERT BAMKIN.
WILLIAM FOSTER.

Richard Bullock, Chairman of Hucknall Urban District Council, presents a book to Harry Sharp on his retirement, March 1974. A native of Stockton-on-Tees, Mr Sharp began work in a solicitors office and after service in the Second World War was employed by Walton and Weybridge Urban District Council, moving to Hucknall to take up the post of Town Clerk which he filled with efficiency for twenty-eight years.

Fundraising for the Hucknall National School, c.1920. Canon Barber demonstrates his skill with the barrel organ. Second from left is the dapper Eric Johnstone, who always worked enthusiastically for school and church.

Baptist church elders outside the Watnall Road premises, c.1958. Back row: R. Teed, ? Culverhouse, Geoffrey Clay. Second row: Harry Morley, extreme left, and Wilson Buck, centre. Hannah Cook is the lady standing on the left.

Hucknall parish church is the proud possessor of no less than nine bells. One is medieval and is hung separately so it does not ring with the peel. This informal snapshot was taken outside the parish church when the bells were returned to the town after recasting by Messrs John Taylor and Co. of Loughborough in the early 1960s. The names inscribed on various bells are those of Henry Morley Raynor (1885–1951), Kenneth Thompson, vicar, church wardens Kenneth W. Reed and George A. Truscott, and Theophilvs Allcock, church warden in 1749.

Canon Barber received a car as his retirement gift from the people of the town in 1946. Canon Thomas Gerrard Barber was incumbent priest at Hucknall parish church for forty-two years. Much loved and respected, his lasting gift to the town was his book *Byron and Where he is Buried* detailing the search for Saxon artefacts and the opening of the family tomb in 1938. His successor, Kenneth Thompson, stands on the left of the picture.

This postcard, showing the Chancel of Hucknall parish church, was addressed to Henry Morley, Dispatch Office, Hucknall, and the post-date was 25 January 1931, Margate. Part of the message reads 'kindly note new address is No. 42 St Peters Road' but was unsigned.

Clergy managers, teachers and children gather to celebrate 100 years of sound Christian education at the National School between 1854 and 1954 in Hucknall. On the extreme left stands Kenneth G. Thompson, then vicar of Hucknall, and later to become first Bishop of Sherwood. Third from the left stands Kittie Calladine who served as School Governor for a great number of years. Fourth from the left is Kenneth W. Reed, headmaster, who served church and school with remarkable leadership and skill.

38

An informal family photograph showing the much respected Joseph (Joe) Sharman, headmaster for many years of Beardall Street Secondary Boys' school. Kind in nature but a firm disciplinarian, many local boys have much to thank him for, as he guided them through their formative years. The picture shows Mr Sharman on the left, his daughter Francis on the far right and Mrs Norah Sharman to her right.

Opposite above: Wards School House, Annesley Road. Built in 1826, the domicile of the headmasters of Hucknall National School was demolished in the 1990s to make way for private housing.

Opposite below: Celebrating the opening of the extension of Hucknall National School in 1911.

Butlers Hill Boys' School, Group 2, 1907. The only known name in this picture is John Jayes, the seventh boy from the left, top row.

National School staff, 1914. Mr Jacklin, headmaster, is the only gentleman in the picture. Seated in the front row is Miss Fieldhouse. Miss Fieldhouse was appointed mistress in charge of the school infant depatment in 1887; a position she was to hold until 1927.

Hucknall National School crowning of the May Queen, 1928.

Hucknall National School, 1a infants class, 1932.

Hucknall National School, the fourth-year leaving class of 1948. The headmaster at this time was Kenneth Walker Reed who took up the position in 1944 and remained for thirty years. He was the last headmaster to live in the school house (now demolished) which has been the headmaster's residence since 1824.

Hucknall National School. An infant class in 1915, Miss Fieldhouse stands on the left.

Hucknall National School, 1b infant class, 1932.

Three

Work and Industry

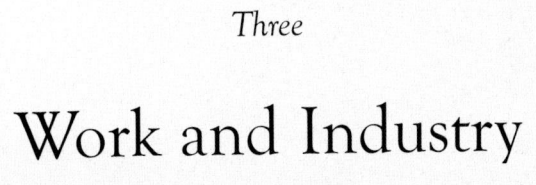

Above: Owner and staff of the Hucknall Manufacturing Company in 1900. Top, from left to right, -?-, Billy Humphries, ? Hodgkinson, -?-, J. Butler, W. Hardstaff, -?-, George Humphries, -?-, Sam Spencer, C. Critchley. Second Row, -?-, S.A. Calladine, W.J. Calladine, ? Radford, ? Wagg, -?-, -?-. Front row: F. Gee, H. Riley, W. Calladine, M.Calladine, S.A. Severn, -?-.

Left: Mr Bill Stevenson, last of the hand-frame knitters in Hucknall, at work on his machine at J. Buck & Sons Limited. He lived at Aspley and was the last secretary of the United Wool Shawl Fall and Antimacassar Union of Hucknall and District, which functioned for seventy years and had as one of its objectives the maintenance of standards of quality in the industry. Another was that the men should never work to set hours. Mr Stevenson's father and grandfather were also framework knitters.

Above: Part of the former Hucknall Water Works at the Salterford site. It was not until 1881 that Hucknall had its own water supply, when the population of the town stood at 10,023. The pumping engines worked 120 hours per week and raised 233,000 gallons a day. The average daily consumption at that time was 14 gallons per head.

Right: Hucknall Torkard postmen photographed outside the old High Street post office opposite the top of Albert Street. No names are known but the name H. Cook is written on the bottom of the picture. The Penny Post was introduced in 1840 when a letter from London to Hucknall cost an old 10p.

Left: Hucknall postman William Hill, who lived on Montague Road. The style of uniform indicates that the period was prior to the First World War.

Below: F.J. Bamkins' machine room in 1937. The girls were employed as knitters and toe seamers.

Jack Bamkin, in braces, with an unknown employee in the warehouse at the firm's original premises on Portland Road. Jack Bamkin died in the 1960s.

Jack and employee again, in what was then the new boiler room at the Portland Road premises.

Factories of Richard Wright and Viyella, formerly William Hollins, on Caddaw Avenue. Sadly no more, having given way to housing.

Hucknall Co-operative Society Board of Directors, 1964. From left to right: G. Bools, Dennis Booth, G. Manning, Frank Johns, A. Cross, W. Allen, C. Meek, A. Kirk, Doug Otter, C. Willet, Mrs M. Turton, Mrs B. Patterson, F. Sterland, F. Whyatt.

Hucknall No. 2 Colliery, bottom pit car park. The car on the extreme left is thought to be a Ford Cortina.

Above: The old Hucknall No. 1 Colliery on Watnall Road opened in 1861 and closed in 1943. This view from the colliery yard fades away to the Misk Hills.

Left: The manager explains. Hucknall-born William (Bill) Elliott, on the left of the picture, started work as a stable lad on leaving school at fourteen, eventually rising through the ranks to be given the prestigious appointment of manager of the then newly-opened Calverton Colliery. A popular and likeable man, he represented the town of Hucknall at cricket and water polo.

All aboard for the coal face. This happy group are being transported to work below ground at Calverton Colliery, c.1962.

Above: Linby Colliery in 1959. This picture shows the right tail gate (north return) in the high main seam.

Right: Work over for the day. Grimy and weary miners emerge from the pit cage into the sunlight.

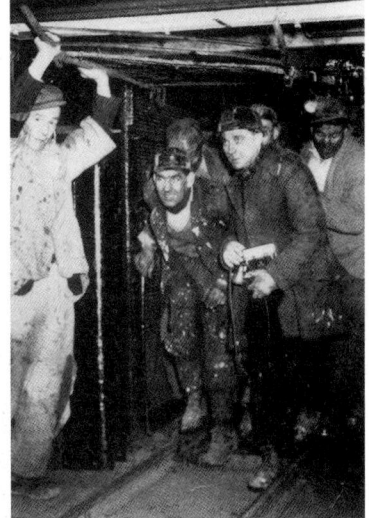

Opposite above: A surface view of Linby Colliery during alterations and reconstruction in 1963.

Opposite below: Linby Colliery as it was in the late 1960s.

Hucknall No. 1 Colliery Pit Tower. Not the leaning tower of Pisa but the Colliery Foreman leaning into the picture!

Washing away the dust. Work over, these miners enjoy a joke and a hot shower at the pit head baths before leaving for home.

Four

Events and Personalities

A group of senior citizens at the Homes of Rest, Park Drive in 1937. Opened in 1926 the Homes were the gift of Sir Julian Cahn.

Heavy snow in the winter of 1942 led to German and Italian prisoners of war who were billeted in the area being brought in to clear the Midland Line railway track.

A budding photographer. A young Harry Morley, eldest son of *Dispatch* owner Henry Morley, prepares for a later career with the family newspaper.

NOTTINGHAM CORPORATION TRAMWAYS

EMPLOYEES' INSTITUTE.

GRAND CONCERT

In aid of the Funds of the above, will be given in

CIRCUS ✻ STREET ✻ HALL,

Thursday, March 22nd, 1906.

ARTISTES:—

MISS BESSIE MAUDE, MISS RACHEL HODGETT,

MR. A. W. KINGSTON, MR. W. HOLLAND,

MR. A. ROWLAND, (Tramways Staff), MR. A. HIRST (Tramways Staff),

THE BYRON QUARTET.

Messrs. A. W. Kingston, W. T. Kingston, W. T. Holland, and H. G. M. Henderson.

Accompanist - - - *MR. F. HOPKINSON.*

DOORS OPEN 7.15. CONCERT 7.45.

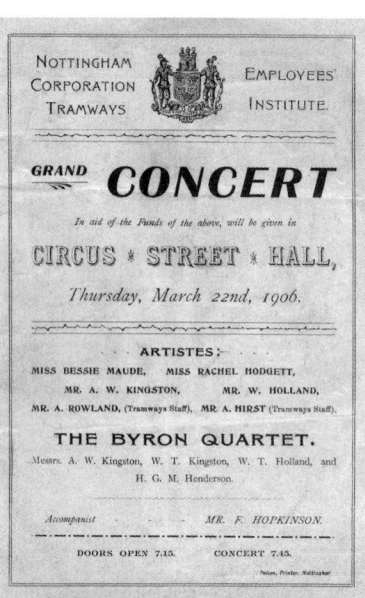

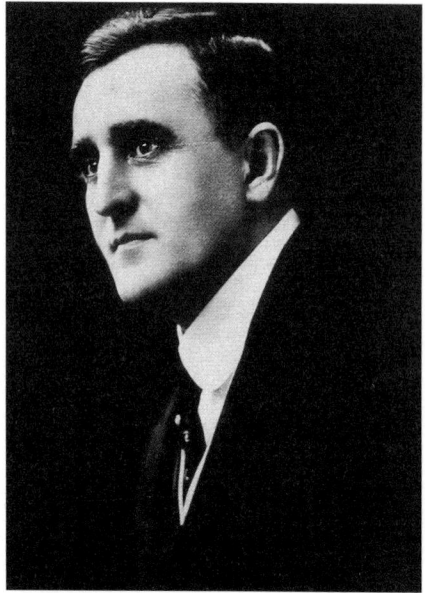

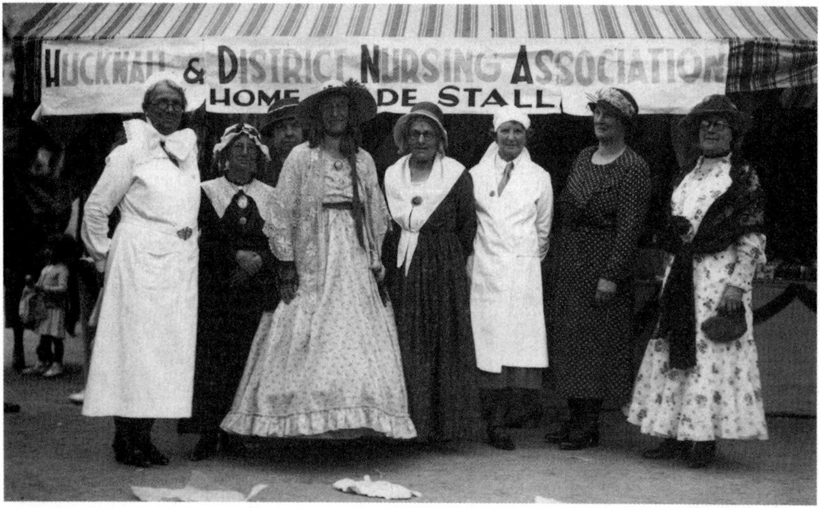

Bamkins family and staff in fancy dress man the home-made stall to raise funds for the Hucknall and District Nursing Association.

A Bamkin family wedding. F.J. Bamkin, father of the bride, is seated with the dog on his lap. Sarah Bamkin is on his right. Sarah was responsible for the foundation of this old established Hucknall firm in 1886, using her husbands name who had nothing to do with the manufacture of socks. He was an engine wright, having come to Hucknall to work at the newly-sunk pit. At the outset all the work on socks was done by out-workers until the original factory was built on Portland Road. Demand for the products created a need for more manufacturing space and a few years ago the Jaegar Works in the town were purchased where the firm thrives today under the leadership of Managing Director Andrew Hamilton, great grandson of Sarah.

Opposite above, left: The Byron Quartet were well known and in much demand in the County of Nottinghamshire during the early 1900s. This programme shows that the Quartet performed *Wake then O Darling* while A.W. Kingston, soon to become Morgan Kingston, sang *Roses* by Adams.

Opposite above, right: Morgan Kingston 'The Singing Coal Miner'. Born in 1876 he attended Beardall Street School, a few yards from his Hucknall home. On leaving school he obtained work at Hucknall Colliery where the mine owner Edward Ellis encouraged his singing talents, giving him time off from work to study Music and Italian. At the age of twenty-four he launched his full-time operatic career. Within a few years he became a leading dramatic tenor. At the New York Metropolitan Opera House he performed all the great operas alongside the great Enrico Caruso, while the critics proclaimed him 'The Greatest Manrico' in the world of opera at that time. He died in 1936 aged sixty-two and is buried in the cemetery at Stoke Poges.

Happy F.J. Bamkin staff photographed at the rear of their Portland Road premises, c.1920.

A trip to the East Coast during the summer was an annual event for Bamkin's office staff and workers. This picture was taken at Mablethorpe in the late 1920s.

Harry Hibbert Bamkin (1866–1932). For many years he ran the company along with his sister, Cecilia Dixon (*née* Bamkin). Harry also had an interest in a local estate agency.

Above: Three generations of the Bullock family, the town's photographers. For many years any event worthy of note in the town was recorded on film by three generations of the Bullock family. The firm was founded in 1902 by P.A. Bullock (centre) and traded in Hucknall High Street for eighty-seven years. After his death in 1926 his son, the late Claude Bullock pictured on the left, took over the business. Claude died in 1967 having left his mark as a first-class photographer and famous for entering the Byron Tomb in 1938 as official photographer of a select group to record in pictures—a unique and historic occasion. The late Deryck Bullock (right) with foresight retained the photographic business but expanded into toys, the towns first self-service shop trading with great success. Deryck's untimely death at the age of fifty-nine led to the sale of the property by his wife Joan. A service to the town greatly missed.

Opposite above: British Legion Garden Party at the Elms in 1948. A demure Ann Morley presents Winifred Duchess of Portland with a bouquet of flowers. Revd K.G. Thompson, left, and Wilf Reynolds (standing) look on approvingly.

Opposite below: One of Hucknall's first motor cars, reputedly owned by Henry (Harry) Smithurst. On the extreme left stands Henry Morley, while the driver (unknown) is being welcomed with great amusement by Mr Harry Johnes.

Above: Pupils and tutors of the Romney Studio of Speech and Drama situated on Station Road, Hucknall, in the 1960s. Front left is Ann Tyler, the boy on the right is thought to be Philip Moss, while in the back row are Mr and Mrs Blackwood, principals, with Sheila Hall and Penelope Kinch.

Left: George 'Digger' Nixon at the Hucknall Boys' Brigade Camp at Bridlington in the 1940s. Steward at the Lads' Club on Watnall Road, he was both friend and guide to scores of Hucknall boys during their membership of the 18th Nottingham Boys' Brigade Company. At annual summer camps he was Quarter Master and cook. This picture, taken outside his tent, displays an ample supply of Smiths crisps.

Right: Jack Blagden poses outside his shop on Derbyshire Lane. He was severely injured in the First World War whilst attempting to escape from his German captors. Nevertheless he enjoyed a successful business and social life. During the Second World War he supplied the country's servicemen and women by supplying comfort funds for the Forces.

Below: British Legion at the Elms shortly after the Second World War. Seated fifth from the left is Bert Buzzard. On his left is Lt-Col. Chaworth Musters. Fourth from the left, standing, is Cis Bennington and sixth from the left is the Revd K.G. Thompson. Standing second from the right is Tom Hanson while third from the right, seated, is Walter Wagg.

Left: Reuben Bramley of Hucknall. A general factotum, he did picture framing, sign writing, illuminated addresses as well as being an all-round entertainer, often appearing as Professor Bee R.A. His shop was next door to Toy Allcocks on the High Street. His brother, Tom Bramley, a butcher, was in trade next door.

Below: The retirement of Eric Morley from his journalistic career in 1976. Col. Tom Forman Hardy presents a silver salver to Eric, whilst William Forman Hardy smiles approvingly, surrounded by fellow directors of the *Nottingham Evening Post*.

Opposite above: Hucknall Rotary Club members and their ladies in the 1960s. Back row, second left, is Harold Calladine, fourth left Cyril Taylder followed by George Wass, Mr Proctor, Dick Howitt, J. Haywood, -?-, Arthur Draper , -?-, Henry Morley, third left standing Jack Stallard then Kittie Calladine, -?-, Stella Taylder, Mrs C. Taylder, -?-, Mrs Bamkin, -?-, Sylvia Howitt, Albert Neil seated, Wilf Reynolds, fourth from right Mrs Haywood.

Soldiers of the King's Royal Rifle Corp photographed whilst on service in South Africa during the Boer War. Sam Brailsford of Hucknall, born in 1869, is the hatted soldier on the extreme right of the picture. He was employed as a postman prior to army service and returned to that occupation on demobilisation. He lived with Mr and Mrs Hill on Montague Road.

The White family of Hucknall in the 1920s. Remarkable then as they were all over six feet tall, but not quite so unique today. Top row: Charles White, Tom White, William White. Bottom row: Fred White, Arthur White, Harry White.

Left: Hucknall Carnival, 1930s. One of Frank Sisson's contributions. Johnnie Knight is the Jack Tar towering above the rest.

Opposite above: This was the scene at Hucknall Library during the 1986 centenary celebrations of the birth of local composer Eric Coates. Eric Coates' son, Austin, bottom left back view, enthralled an invited audience as he reminisced about his father and his music. He endeared himself by telling them 'Friends said to me "I suppose you will be in London for your fathers centenary celebrations?" "No," I replied "I shall be in Hucknall because that is where my father would want me to be."'

The Ladies Section of the Hucknall Co-operative Junior Choir, serenading the Revd Tom Irvine and his wife Jean on the occasion of their wedding reception at the Commodore Banqueting Suite on 29 December 1962. Paul Lobb, the long-serving accompanist, can be seen in the background.

Henry (Harry) Smithurst was one of Hucknalls' early entrepreneurs, commencing work at the age of eight as a stocking hand. Later becoming a Shetland shawl and lace manufacturer and designer, he owned factories in Byron Street, Spring Street and High Street. Eventually he went to Russia to set up a shawl factory and made his fortune. He later returned to Hucknall, and built and owned houses in Victoria Street and Queen Street, living with his family at Haddon House. He was one of the first people in Hucknall to own a motor car. He died in 1940, two weeks short of his ninety-second birthday. Back row: Henry Smithurst and Ada Herrod (granddaughter). Front row: Elizabeth Herrod (daughter) and Annie Holmes (daughter).

A group of Hucknall business men and women, thought to be in the 1940s. Among those photographed are E. Breedon, C. Taylder, G. Claxton, W. Taylder, M. Holehouse, G. Willis, O. Wilcockson, H. Morley, Mr DeForge, Mr Harmon, Mrs Claxton, Mrs Willis, C. Bullock.

Five
Sports and Leisure in the District

Hucknall Collieries Football Club. This photograph shows the colliery junior side with their impressive array of trophies. From left to right, back row: John Peck, Frank Worrall, Gerald Sharrard, David Jones, A. Johnson, Gordon Petcher. Seated: Keith Cowell, Frank Breedon, Dennis Butler, Ken Williams, David Flatt. On Dennis Butler's right is Bill Morrell and on his left is Bill Elliott, both Colliery Managers. The photograph also shows Harold Down, first left kneeling, with Frank Down immediately behind him. These two brothers have served the Hucknall Team (now Town) for fifty years as players, secretary, team selectors and coach, never losing their enthusiasm for the game.

Son emulates father by taking part in and winning the Notts FA School football competition. Richard Darrington proudly displays his 1985 medal while his father, local sportsman Jack Darrington, holds his medal won in 1953. The Willett Shield was a prestigious trophy awarded to the winners of the Notts FA Schools' Football Tournament.

Right: Gill Restall of Newstead village described by journalists as 'Queen of the Green'. Gill was taught to play bowls by her late father and mother when she was little more than a toddler. 1961 saw her start her competitive career. Gill won her first national title in 1973, winning the National Two Woods EBF Championship. Twenty-five years later, along with daughter Jane Croxall and Betty Binch, she captured the E.B.F. Two Wood Ladies Rink Title. The intervening years have seen Gill take three other national titles and feature in The County Honours List in the 1960s, 1970s, 1980s and 1990s. A past President of the Notts County Bowls Association, Gill continues to promote the game and still plays to an extremely high standard.

Below: The founding of Linby Colliery FC, 1946, then competing in the Notts Spartan League with two permitted ex-football league players. After winning the Spartan League at the first attempt they progressed to the Notts Alliance, thence to full professional status in the Central Alliance. Back row: L. Capewell, W. England, W. Thornley, R. Dulson, the elegant Granville (Swat) Nixon, Fred Williams, Ron Butters, R. Issett (kneeling), Frank Brandham, Ernest (Tim) Coleman, Ken Wright.

Above: Gatehouse Ground, 1950. George Drury scores with a penalty kick against Nuneaton Borough to take Linby Colliery into the first round proper of the FA Cup. After a fine Cup run Linby lost to Third Division opponents Gillingham 4-1. Behind George is player manager Tim Coleman whilst son-in-law Eric Lummus looks anxiously on.

Left: 11 March 1936. Local man Jack Green played the legendary twenty-four-year-old Horace Lindrum of Australia who came to the Church Hall, Hucknall, to demonstrate how snooker should be played. It turned out rather differently—Jack beat the World Champion over three frames winning two of the three Rubbers.

Enid Bakewell of Newstead village—a remarkable cricket talent. The only woman cricket player to feature in *Wisden's Cricket Almanac*, 1968-69, selected for England to tour Australia and New Zealand on her first Senior Tour. She took 118 wickets and scored 1,052 runs making her the first woman player to achieve the double. She first played for young England as a nineteen-year-old. In 1973 she played for England in the first Women's World Cup playing Australia in the final and herself scoring 118 runs. Regularly selected for England and in 1979 at Edgbaston against the West Indians, she batted through the second innings scoring 112 not out and took 10 wickets in the match, being on the field all day. After touring Australia and New Zealand in 1982 Enid retired from international cricket to take up a coaching appointment in London and was made an England selector.

Hazel Grove cricketers at their prize-giving celebrations after winning the Spencer Cup. The team won the trophy in three successive years: 1952, 1953 and 1954. On the extreme right, seated, is the popular and talented Gerald Rostance. From left to right, front row: Maurice Shaw, Tom Wass, Harry Bonser (Secretary), Harry Raynor (President), Mr Willett. Back row, extreme left, stands Fred Stokes, his brother Roland is on the extreme right. John Willett stands behind the Cup.

Butlers Hill School boys' team 1948/49. From left to right, back row: Tony Marriott, John Kendall, Arthur Fern, Mick Stone, John North, Peter Lycett, Roy Calladine. Seated: Roy Burton, John Wigginton, John Wheat, Sid Parker, Terry Beasley, Tony Jayes.

The day the footballers came to Hucknall. Team mates of local football legend Bob Marshall came to Hucknall Parish church for the wedding of his daughter Joan to local sportsman Philip Smith. Matt Busby, the famous football manager, team mate and neighbour of Bob during their Manchester City playing days, along with other members of the successful team of the 1930s attended. The picture outside the Parish church shows the bride and groom, Bob Marsall, Matt Busby, Sam Cowan and the best man Frank Knight of Hucknall, who played and coached at Nottingham Forest for thirty-six years.

Opposite below: Local cricketer Kevin Cooper is pictured here with the County Championship Cup in 1981. Though born in Sutton-in-Ashfield, he has lived in Hucknall all his life. He made his debut for Notts in 1976, aged nineteen years. Described as the 'Master of Line and Length' he left Notts for Gloucester in the early 1990s. His first-class career brought him 2,484 runs and 817 wickets.

Top right: Hucknall-born Peter Harvey of Papplewick Lane. He played for Hucknall Cricket Club under the captaincy of Cecil Rhodes, and made his debut for his county in 1947 in a career that lasted eleven years. He scored 3,645 runs and took 335 wickets. On retirement from cricket he accepted a directorship with Redmayne and Todd–then the leading sports outfitters in the Midlands. Now eighty years of age, he lives at Oadby in Leicestershire.

Middle right: Yorkshire-born Freddie Stocks lived in Hucknall for most of his life. Another member of Hucknall Cricket Club who made the step into the Notts County Team. A likeable and friendly person, Freddie retired to live at Sutton-on-Sea. In a first-class career that spanned twelve years he scored more than 11,000 runs.

Bottom: King George V was in Nottingham to open the new University buildings when he visited Trent Bridge during the Notts match against the West Indian Tourists in 1928. Here his Royal Highness shakes hands with Hucknall resident Bill Voce.

Above: County Junior Tennis Champion Vicki Plews (*née* Smith), formally of Hucknall, is seen here in her early teens. Granddaughter of the late Eric Morley, she was holder of county titles in Nottinghamshire, Yorkshire, Dorset and Lincolnshire. She is now a professional national lawn tennis coach in Yorkshire.

Opposite above: Harold Larwood demonstrates his grip at the rear of his home in Nuncargate. He is probably the greatest fast bowler of all time. After village cricket in Nuncargate where he was born, he joined Notts County Cricket Club in 1924 where his bowling, along with that of Bill Voce, brought great success to the county over the next decade. Emigrating to Australia in 1949, he returned to his native county as often as possible.

Oposite above: 1977 reunited at Trent Bridge—three legends of cricket born in the Hucknall area: Harold Larwood, Joe Hardstaff, Bill Voce and former Captain of Notts R.T. Simpson.

Bill Voce returns home from the controversial 1932/33 'Body Line' tour of Australia.

Six

Hucknall RAF and Rolls Royce

An exterior photograph of a ceremonial occasion thought to be just prior to the Second World War, taken outside the main hangar at RAF Hucknall.

Above: A film poster publicising *The Dambusters*. A film of national importance being an epic of heroism and invention, showing the evolution of the bomb that bounced on the water.

Right: Hucknall-born composer Eric Coates wrote the music for the film *The Dambusters*, which reached the top ten in music polls and remained there for over a year—the first instrumental to do so. Eric Coates and his wife Phyl share a joke with the inventor of the bouncing bomb, Barnes Wallis, pictured on the right, on the occasion of the RAF concert at the Royal Albert Hall, London, on 7 April 1956.

Opposite below: Police move in to prevent the late Eric Morley photographing a Heinkel (Rolls Royce) which crashed at Watnall in 1938.

The members of 504 Squadron muster in the hanger at the Aerodrome, Hucknall, c.1930. Note the early propeller aeroplanes in the background.

The personnel at RAF Hucknall on Watnall Road were housed in this type of accommodation. Normally the only heating was a solid fuel stove, and the chimneys can be seen quite clearly in this photograph. To many Polish officers and aircrew, this was home during the Second World War. After the War many settled happily in the area.

Airmen's accommodation at Hucknall. The original 504 Squadron was formed in 1928 at RAF Hucknall as a special reserve Squadron. It became part of the Auxiliary Air Force in 1936 and played an important role in the Battle of Britain. It was disbanded at RAF Wymeswold, Leicestershire, in 1957.

This assembly of the Squadron outside the hangars at Hucknall gives some idea of the strength of the unit at that time.

Standing at ease after the service at Hucknall Parish Church. Both RAF personnel and the Salvation Army must have been a hardy lot as few overcoats are in evidence on what looks to be a snow-covered Market Place. The Scala cinema advertises a film starring Boris Karloff.

Members of 504 Squadron on church parade at Hucknall Parish church. Motor cars seem few and far between.

Following page: An official party of local councillors and staff visit Rolls Royce, Hucknall, in the 1960s. On the left of the picture stands Councillor Hayes, then Councillor Smedley (hatted), and Councillor Simms.

Right: This rare picture is the very first photograph to show the 'Flying Bedstead', the forerunner of vertical take-off aeroplanes. This picture was taken by a Nottingham High School pupil— John Morley, aged fourteen, from Farleys Lane while out walking the family dog, c.1950.

Below: The 'Flying Bedstead' again. This time the first official photograph, c.1950.
Above: The same visit as the previous picture showing Geoff Brogan in the foreground—a genial and efficient Chief Health Inspector of Hucknall Urban District Council. Councillor Stan Grainger brings up the rear.

Left: Franz Von Werra was shot down over Kent on 5 September 1940. Captured, he was eventually imprisoned at Grizedale Hall, Derbyshire, from where he escaped posing as a Dutch pilot. He made his way to Hucknall Aerodrome but was caught on the airfield attempting to take off in a Hurricane Fighter. He was transported to Canada where he leapt from a train in the depth of winter and crossed the St Lawrence River to the United States and subsequently back to Germany.

Above: Group Captain Hughes-Chamberlain Wright and Squadron Leader Boniface— respectively Commanding Officer and Station Adjutant at the time of Von Werra's visit to RAF Hucknall.

Right: Hardy Kruger, who portrayed Von Werra in the film *The One That Got Away*.

Von Werra's entry in the visitors' book at the Rolls-Royce works on Hucknall Aerodrome, 21 December, 1940:

NAME	NATIONALITY	ADDRESS	ORDER	TIMES OF ARRIVAL AND DEPARTURE
van Lott	Dutch	Aberdeen	Sici ood (See A.I.D) 09ᵛ	09-10

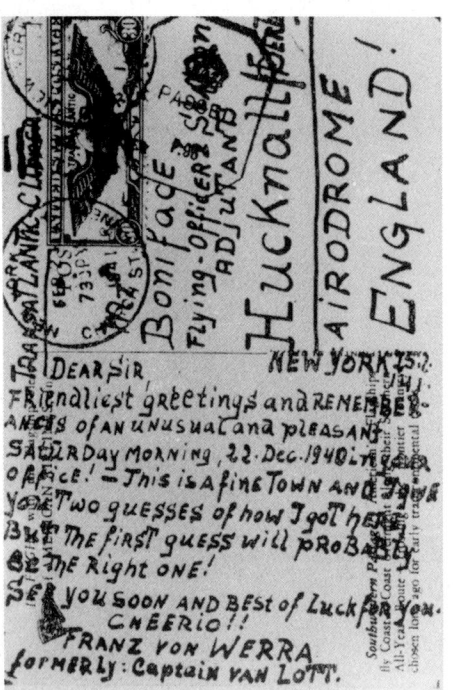

Above: Von Werra's entry in the Visitors Book at the Rolls Royce Works at Hucknall Aerodrome on 21 December 1940.

Left: The postcard which Von Werra sent from the safety of the United States to the Adjutant at Hucknall, recalling their encounter.

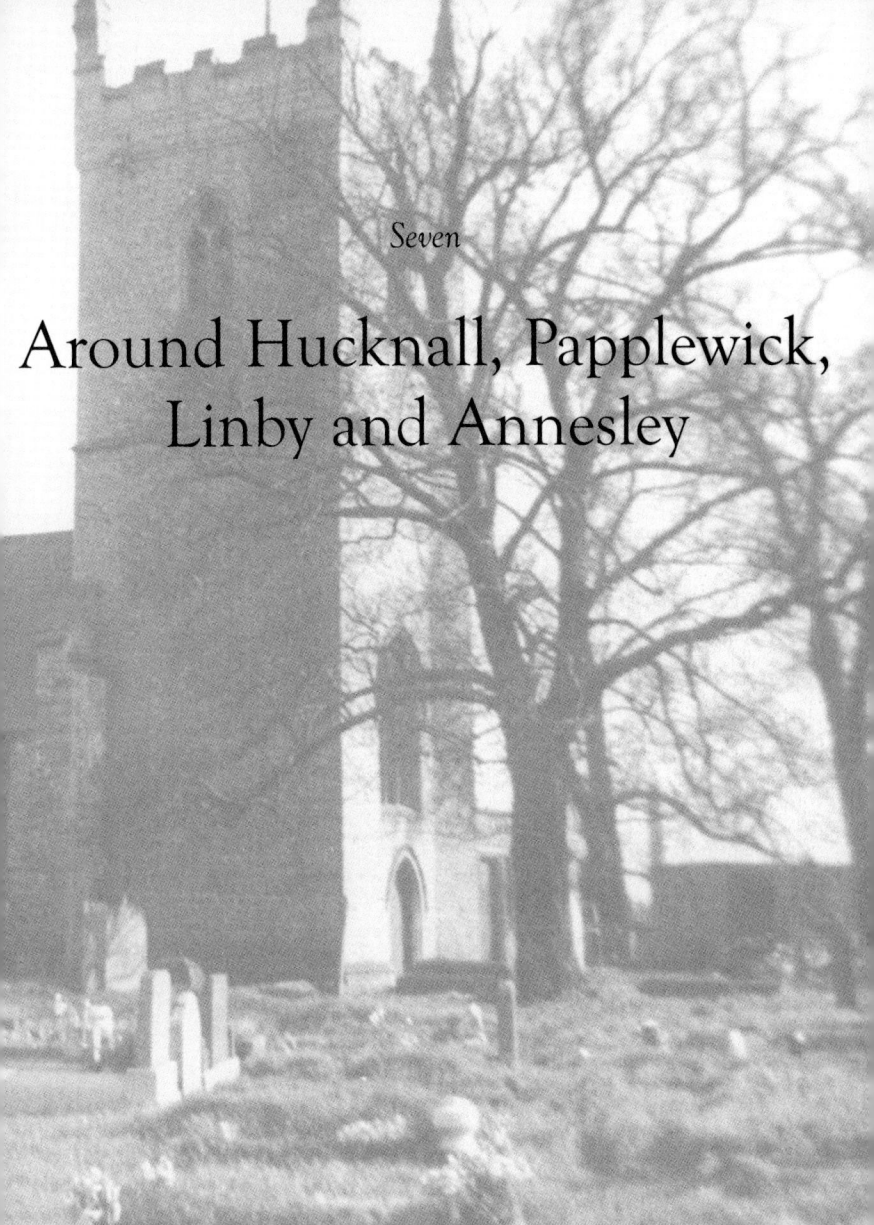

Seven

Around Hucknall, Papplewick, Linby and Annesley

Annesley colliery village, with the pit slag heaps in the background, in the 1950s.

The Lodge Gate House, at the entrance of Annesley Park during demolition in the 1940s. After alterations this stretch of road became and still is one way.

Right: Annesley Hall church, now unused and in disrepair although recent efforts have been made to make the structure safe. It is featured in D.H. Lawrence's *The White Peacock*.

Below: Annesley Hall, the home of Lord Byron's unrequited love Mary Chaworth. The property sadly stands derelict and decaying today.

Annesley Hall—the rear entrance in its heyday.

The door at Annesley Hall showing the bullet holes caused by Lord Byron whilst demonstrating his pistol skills to Mary Chaworth. It was sold when the Hall and its effects were auctioned off, c.1960.

The terrace, Annesley Hall, where the poet Byron strolled with Mary Chaworth.

A social occasion at Annesley Hall, viewed from the terrace in the 1940s.

Above left: Shoulder of Mutton Hill, Annesley, which stands at 610ft above sea level, boasting to be the highest point in Nottinghamshire.

Above right: The Mason and Gray Monuments, erected by William Montague to his friends, the poets Mason and Gray. They were his idols, and in the last year of his life Montague set up two urns in the grounds of Papplewick Hall to commemorate them. On the Linby side of the River Leen was the monument to Gray and on the Papplewick side the one to Mason. In recent times they were vandalised and when an ancestor of William Montague visited the Hall in 1946 he was so upset to see the desecration that he and Mr Claude Chadbourne arranged for the monument to Gray to be removed to Eton College. Now restored it stands as a memorial to former pupils of that school who fell in the Second World War.

All that remains of the Mason Monument in Papplewick Hall Woods, 1992. It has since been removed, restored and resides in private ownership.

Right: Since the closure of the local colliery, Linby has regained much of its old charm. Almost uniquely the village is fortunate to boast two village crosses—'The Top Cross' being recognised as the older of the two. The base is ancient and original, being the only example of a seven-sided base in the country. (David Henshaw)

Below: Linby Parish church.

Old Castle Mill, Linby, showing the old road. The property has been renovated and is now used as private residential accommodation.

Papplewick dam, as it was in 1930 before drainage and road alterations took place. A haven for fishermen and, in severe winters, ice skaters.

Papplewick dam, almost drained of water in preparation for the road scheme to commence.

The cottages at the top of Papplewick village present an idyllic country scene.

Local children enjoy the maypole dancing at Papplewick Hall, then the home of Mr and Mrs Claude Chadbourne. The house was built in Adams Style by Frederick Montague between the years 1781 to 1797.

Cottages in Papplewick village in the 1950s. The village shop under the awning was owned by Mr and Mrs Anderson, and 300 yards further up the street the village post office was run by Mr and Mrs Mills.

Papplewick church was given to the priory of Newstead by Henry II in 1170. Frederick Montague of Papplewick Hall was a generous benefactor to this delightful church. Owen Mealey, the poet Byron's Land Agent is interred in the grounds.

The interior of Papplewick church, photographed by Eric Morley in 1948.

This postcard, posted in August 1908 from Annesley Woodhouse, was addressed to Mrs M. Raynor of No. 82 Derbyshire Lane, Hucknall.

Elizabeth Shepherd of Papplewick left her home on 7 July 1817 to seek employment in Mansfield. Towards evening her mother, having gone to meet her, saw her returning along the road and turned back thinking her daughter would overtake her. She did not, and upon a search her body was discovered laying on the spot near Harlow Wood where this memorial is erected. Hue and cry was raised and a rogue called Charles Rotherham was arrested, tried and duly executed.

Right: A Nelson Column in the autumn woods at Papplewick. The Hon. Frederick Montague of Papplewick erected this column to commemorate Nelson's naval victories. It is now the property of Mr Dennis Cotteril.

Below: For over four years the little village of Linby had a WVS home for blind evacuees. In September 1939 the WVS of Linby and Papplewick found and equipped Lynwoods—a delightful little bungalow—and worked all hours making blackout screens. Not a penny was spent, everything was given or lent. The following day the first guests arrived—three men and two ladies. They remained in the village, enjoying the peace and tranquillity of this quiet village and are buried in the Linby Parish churchyard.

NEAR THIS STONE LIE THE MORTAL REMAINS OF THESE WHO WERE BLIND BROUGHT TO LYNWOOD AND THE SAFETY OF LINBY FROM THE DANGER OF AIR RAIDS. THEY FOUND ETERNAL SANCTUARY.

THOMAS EAGLING. AGED 79 YEARS. DIED MAY 1941.
ELIZABETH WADE. AGED 88 YEARS. DIED SEPT. 1942.
SARAH ANN STOCKS. AGED 90 YEARS. DIED DEC. 1943.
JAMES WILLIAM NELSON. AGED 71 YEARS. DIED JUNE 1944.
WILLIAM STORR. AGED 82 YEARS. DIED MAY 1945.

The old gateway to Linby, Linby Bridge, about to be demolished in July 1993. It originally bridged the Hucknall Town railway line.

Sherwood House, Linby, former home of the late Miss Evelyn Gray, daughter of the owner of Linby Colliery. The house, now redeveloped, provides first-class accommodation which is in trust in the family name.

Eight

Around Hucknall, Newstead and the Abbey

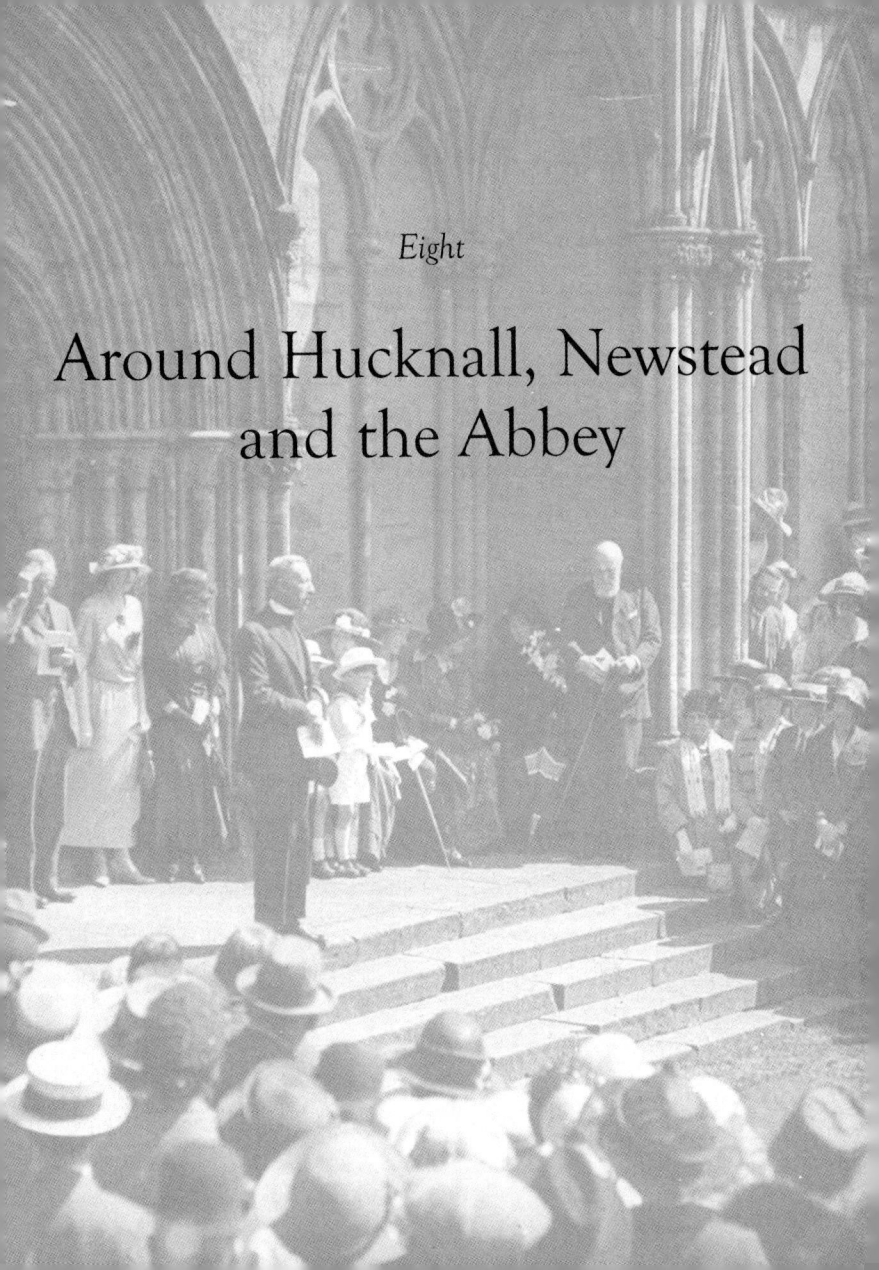

The South Notts Hunt gather at Newstead Abbey in 1920 for their annual Boxing Day meet.

Opposite: William Smith of Hays Farm, Newstead, (1837-1922), grandson of Nanny Smith.

Bill Smith of Woodborough with his wife Joan, great, great grandson of Nanny Smith. Like his grandfather, he has been in farming all his life, firstly on the Newstead Estate and later at Woodborough, where he now lives in retirement.

Rock House, Newstead Abbey, the home of Nanny Smith. Nanny Smith was the housekeeper during the poet's occupancy of Newstead Abbey. When the poet sold the Abbey, her services were no longer required and she went to live in Rock House. From abroad the poet enquired of the new owner, Colonel Wildman, if his old housekeeper was being well cared for. She was immediately housed in more comfortable accommodation. Nanny was a great defender of the poet and strongly contradicted reports that his time at Newstead was spent in licentious ways and drunken orgies.

The view from Rock Cottage, Newstead.

Sophia Hyatt, otherwise known as the White Lady, was an ardent admirer of the poet Byron and lodged here at Weir Mill Farm, Newstead. Photographed around 1925.

Left: Imitation or Folly Castle? Entrance to the ground floor showing '1749' as the date built.

Below: Newstead Abbey became the property of the City of Nottingham in July 1931, the gift of Sir Julien Cahn. Here an unknown cleric addresses the assembled audience.

The gathering at the front of Newstead Abbey in July 1931, when the property was gifted by Sir Julien Cahn.

Above: This rear view gives some idea of the interest shown in the gifting of Newstead Abbey to the City of Nottingham.

Left: Prior to the ceremony at Newstead Abbey, the Greek President Venizelos attended a service at Hucknall Parish church to pay tribute to the poet Lord Byron. Here the president's valet holds a floral tribute from Greek residents who lived in England.

In May 1927 the Revd Lord Byron came to Newstead Abbey to open the Sale of Work and fête. He is seen here addressing the crowd.

Mrs Fraser, the then owner of Newstead Abbey, welcomes a distinguished company at the Sale of Work and fête at her home.

Left: Thomas Leonard 'Len' Turton of Newstead Village was born 6 March 1898. Len Turton's love and concern for his village and his involvement with local government earned him the nickname 'Mayor of Newstead' an apt title considering the assiduous work he did for this former mining village. He retired from colliery work in 1963 having been a trade unionist all his life. For his eminent and public services he was admitted to be an Honorary Freeman of the Borough of Gedling in 1976. His only daughter is Miss Enid Bakwell who captained the English Ladies' Cricket Team on numerous occasions.

Below: Byron memorabilia pictured at Newstead Abbey at the time of the Webb family occupancy.

Above: The Eagle Pond at Newstead Abbey, named after the lectern that was recovered many years after having been deposited there at the time of the dissolution of the Abbey. The lectern now stands in Southwell Minster.

Right: The Ragged Rock, which stands at the head of Sherwood Lake at Newstead. Its constructor, the Firth Lord Byron, intended to double the lake size and the Ragged Rock on the western side should have risen from the centre of the water. Virtual bankruptcy prevented him from completing the scheme.

Interior of Folly Castle showing remains of the old school desks once occupied by the children of the estate workers, c.1920.

More Byron relics, shown here in 1916.

Nine

Around Hucknall, Bulwell and Beauvale Abbey

Beauvale Priory as seen and painted in oils by Elias Lacey of Hucknall. Elias Lacey was a painter and decorator but was more famous for his painting of local scenes. He was originally in business on Hucknall Market Place, where he commissioned the erection of the statue of Lord Byron. He later lived and worked from his home on Derbyshire Lane.

Beauvale Priory. The ruins are all that remain of one of the eight 'Charterhouses' or Carthusian Monasteries which were all that existed in England at the time of the dissolution of the monasteries by Henry VIII.

Right: Watnall Hall was for many years the possession of the Rolleston Family. Its best-known feature was the beautiful wrought iron-gates believed to be the work of Huntingdon Shaw of Nottingham, who was reputably the designer of the magnificent gates at Hampton Court. The Hall is now demolished.

Left: Kirkby Cross in the 1960s, one of Nottinghamshire's ancient crosses. The notice board suggests the picture was taken in 1966.

Right: Colwick Hall, now closed and neglected, was once the home of the poet Byron's Mary. The house was famous for its magnificent mahogany doors, elegant staircase and above all its wonderful fireplaces in multi-coloured marbles in the style of the brothers Adam. The house was severely damaged by Reform Bill rioters from Nottingham in 1831.

Marshall of Bulwell founded in 1930, were synonymous with national and international transportation. Founded by Rex Marshall—here checking the stock on one of his very first vehicles—the firm prospered and made steady growth and was nationalised after the Second World War. After de-nationalisation the firm was restored to the Marshall Family. Rex Marshall, assisted by his two sons Howard and Trevor, turned the business into a massive enterprise. After the death of their father and retirement of the two sons, the twelve-acre site came up for development and is now a retail park.

Marshall's main office on the Hucknall to Bulwell Road. The family home is on the right. As the firm expanded even this was taken over for further office accommodation.

The Marshall site pictured from the rear. Bulwell Export and Packing was a subsidiary of A.R. Marshall & Sons and transported goods to all parts of the world. The embankment of the Nottingham to Sheffield railway line can be seen in the background.

The security guard. Note how the dog checks in a driver to the Marshall Depot. The firm was the first major company in the area to use dogs as part of their security measures.

Bulwell Wood Hall, the home of John Byron of Clayton and Lord William the Third, before he succeeded to the peerage.

Bulwell Wood Hall in the 1950s shortly before demolition, after vandals, then a fire, decided its future.

Bulwell Wood Hall, prior to demolition.

Bestwood Furnaces. For forty years the red glow lit up the sky to the north of Nottingham. Bestwood Furnaces produced pig-iron until the plant was closed down in 1928. The site consisted of five steel brick-lined kilns standing 60ft high and was not demolished until 1947.

The old Grammar School, or Strelley House, Bulwell, c.1928. It was erected in 1667 by George Strelly of Hempsall for the education of young children and inhabitants of the parish. The schoolmaster was exhorted to use his pupils mildly and teach them Latin and accompts. The charity continued its work until 1885 when the school was discontinued and the building sold.

Bulwell from the Market Place in 1860.